Tyrannosaurus (ty-RAN-o-sawr-us) footprints, late Cretaceous

Copyright © 2002, Laurie Shade

All rights reserved. No part of this publication may be reproduced or transmitted in any form or by any means, electronic or mechanical, including photocopy, recording, or any information storage and retrieval system, without permission in writing from the publisher.

Requests for permission to make copies of any part of the work should be mailed to: Copyrights and Permissions Department, The Little Buckeye Publishing Co., P. O. Box 21084, Columbus, Ohio 43221-0084.

First published in the United States of America in 2002 by The Little Buckeye Publishing Co.

Library of Congress Control Number 2001119922

San Number 253-5718

ISBN 0-9703936-1-X

Series 1, Number 2

5 4 3 2 1

Written and Illustrated by
Laurie Shade

Art Production by
DOV Graphics
Cincinnati, Ohio

Printed by
The C.J. Krehbiel Company
Cincinnati, Ohio

A special thanks to Dale Gnidovec, Curator of the Orton Geological Museum at The Ohio State University, for sharing his vast knowledge and insight of dinosaurs.

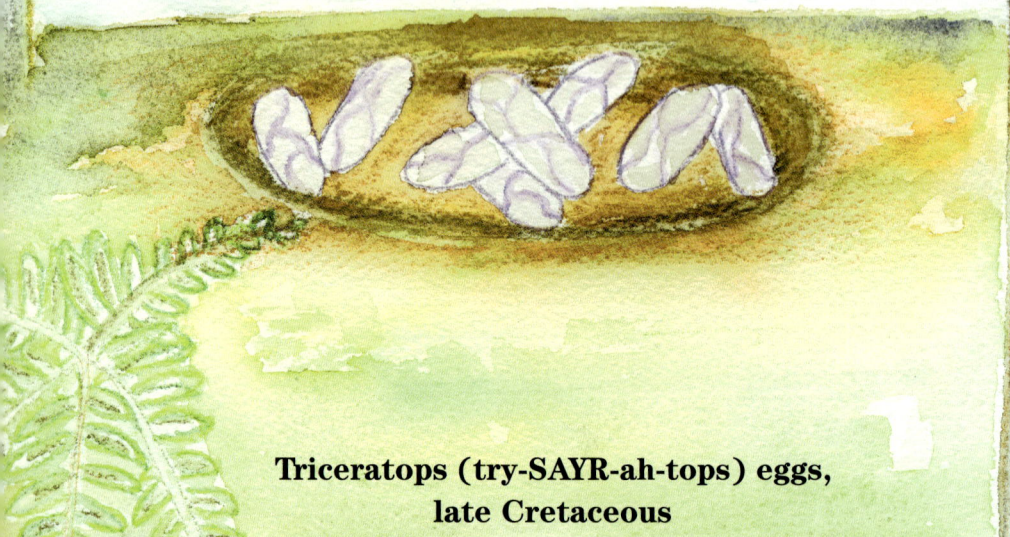

**Triceratops (try-SAYR-ah-tops) eggs,
late Cretaceous**

The Little Buckeye Discovers Dinosaurs

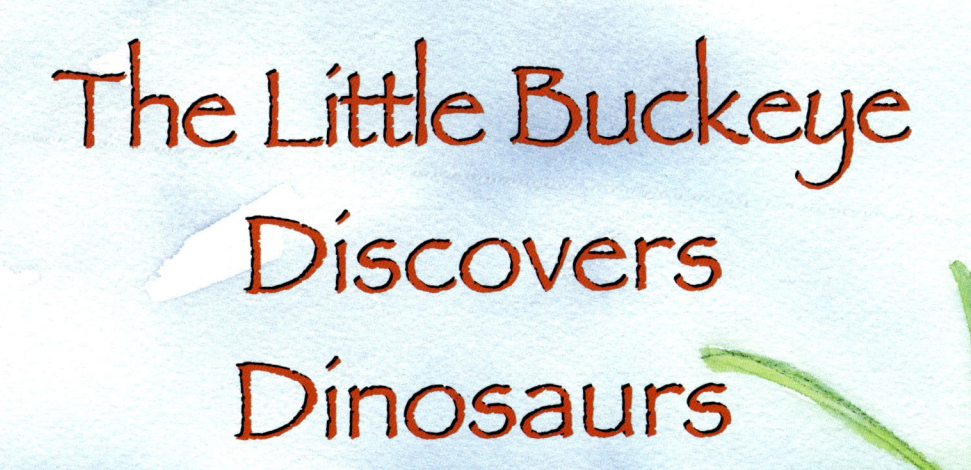

Story and Pictures by
Laurie Shade

Stegosaurus (STEG-o-sawr-us), late Jurassic

For Louis and Sophie

This book belongs to
_____

Parasaurolophus (par-ah-sawr-OL-o-fus) babies, late Cretaceous

Little Buckeye sat quietly. His grandfather, a retired paleontologist, was telling him a story about the dinosaurs that may have lived in Ohio.

Over 320 million years ago,
Ohio was covered by a shallow sea.
There were trilobites and sharks,
and sea anemones.

It was quite a sea to see.

Millions of years passed, the land began to rise. The climate of Ohio was nice, warm and dry.

The dinosaurs emerged, each more spectacular than the next. There were meat eaters and plant eaters; they had to co-exist.

The meat eating dinosaurs had sharp teeth. They had strong muscular back legs and were quick on their feet.

Other dinosaurs such as Anchisaurus (ANG-kee-sawr-us) may have eaten plants and meat. They had light weight bones and long slender feet.

Rutiodon (ROOT-ee-o-don) was not a dinosaur at all, but a meat eating reptile. He lived in streams and lakes and ate smaller animals, like delicious cupcakes.

Coelophysis (see-lo-FYS-iss) traveled in packs, running swiftly to avoid attack.

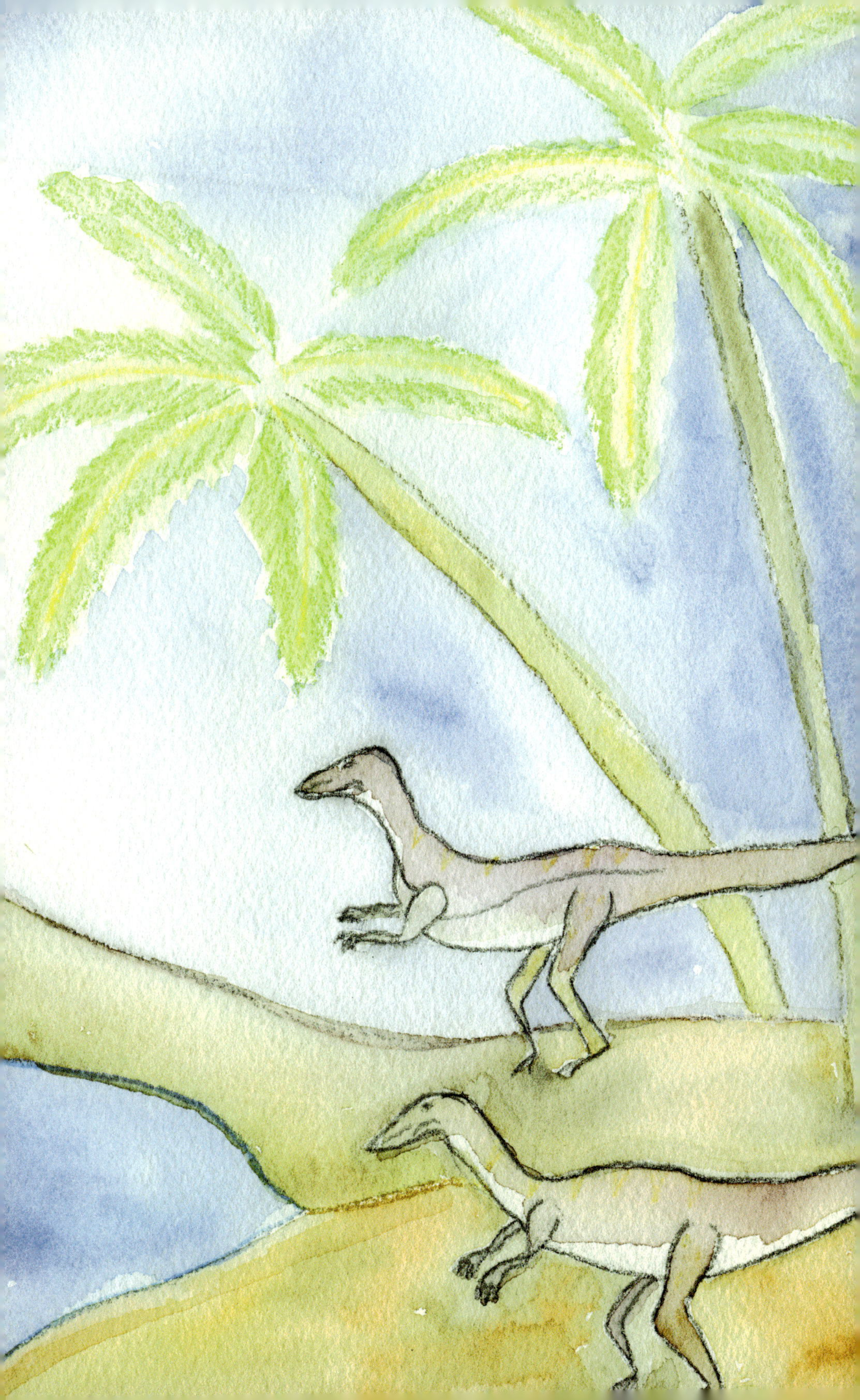

Ammosaurus (AM-o-sawr-us) and her baby wandered from the herd. They came upon many green, leafy trees, and munched on all they could.

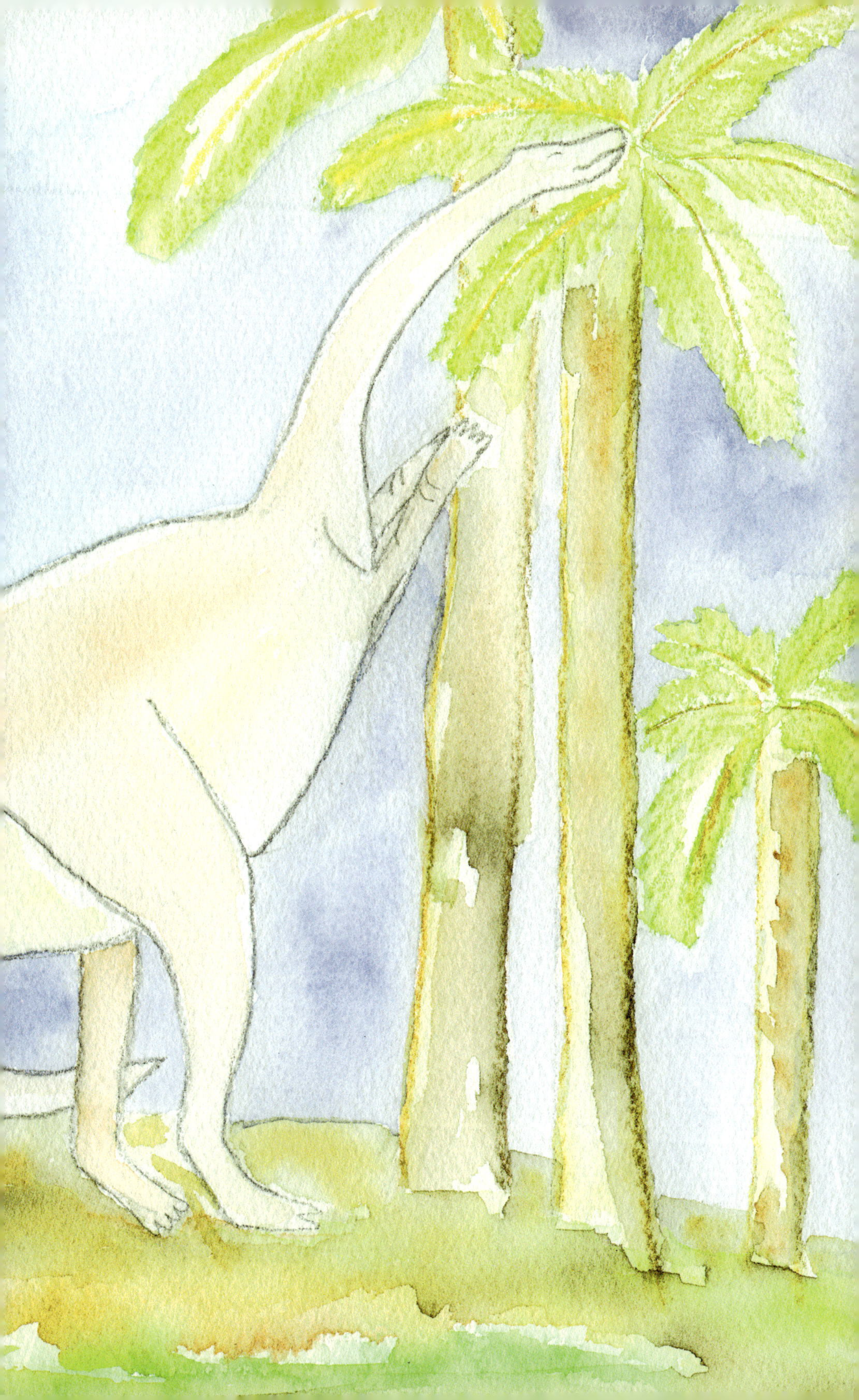

The Jurassic Period was upon them;
adaptation was a must.
The dinosaurs changed shape;
they were more diverse, more robust.

Apatosaurus (ah-PAT-o-sawr-us)
and Allosaurus (AL-o-sawr-us);
their names both start with A.
The former was an herbivore;
the latter stalked its prey.

Nanosaurus (NAN-o-sawr-us) loved to eat horse tails. They were tasty, tasty good. Diplodocus (dih-PLOD-o-kus) was a dinosaur of immense length. The ground shook when he walked, and sank where he stood.

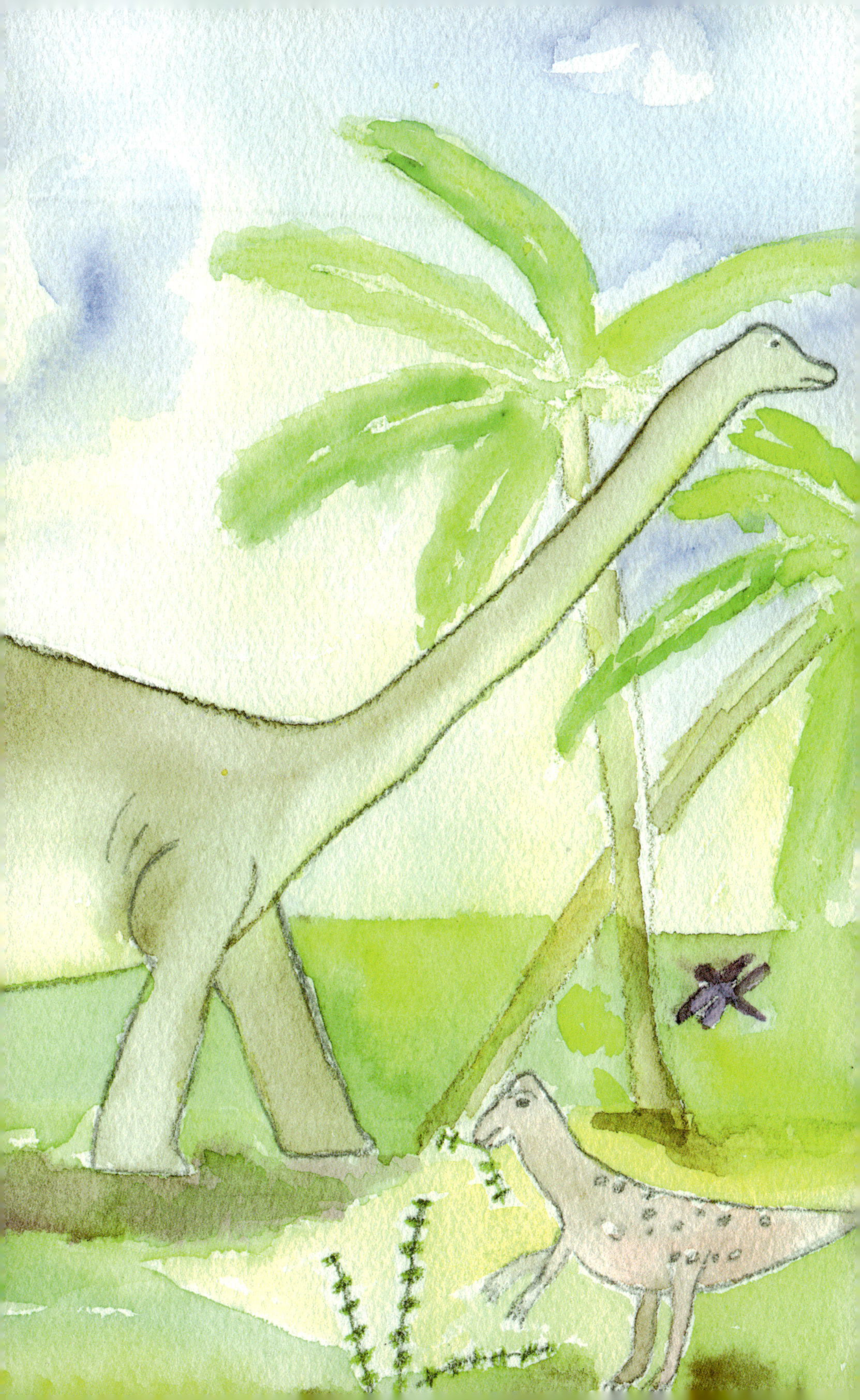

Crunch, crunch, munch munch. Camptosaurus
(KAMP-to-sawr-us) did eat a bunch.
An ancestor of the duckbilled dinosaurs;
their hands had five fingers,
and they walked on all fours.

Stegosaurus (STEG-o-sawr-us) was an interesting fellow, with jagged back and colors of yellow. He stood in the sunshine and warmed his plates; they were his temperature regulator, and helped him attract a mate.

**The last period of the Mesozoic Era,
the Cretaceous Period it is said to be,
where the dinosaurs were enormous,
ferocious, and incredibly beautiful to see.**

The trees were as tall as clouds.
Pteranodon (tayr-AN-o-don) glided
up and down. While much farther
below, a family of Triceratops
(try-SAYR-ah-tops) played with
their young, trying to tip over a tree...
ah, what fun.

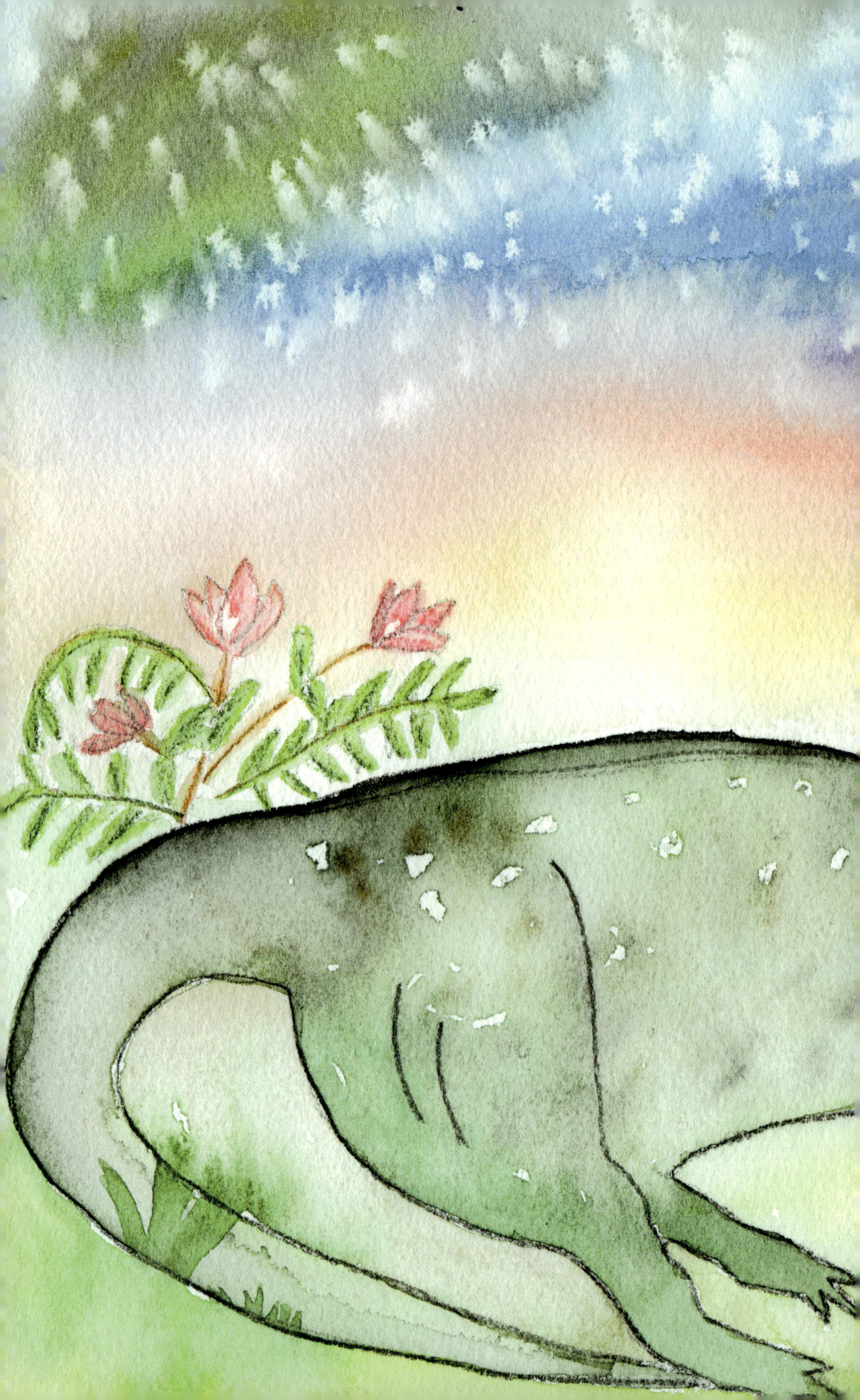

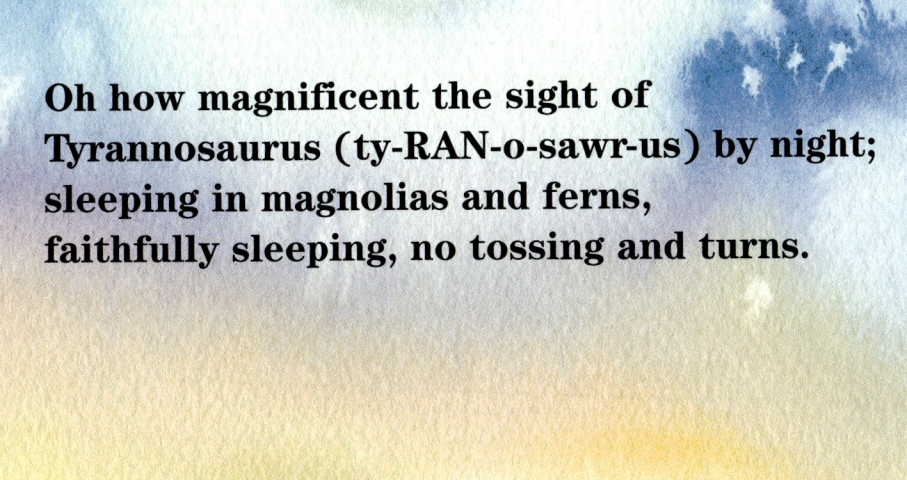

Oh how magnificent the sight of Tyrannosaurus (ty-RAN-o-sawr-us) by night; sleeping in magnolias and ferns, faithfully sleeping, no tossing and turns.

Parasaurolophus (par-ah-sawr-OL-o-fus) sang in the morning dawn; others gathered to hear his mating song.

Pachycephalosaurs (pak-ee-sef-ah-lo-SAWR-us) began to prance; they came together and parted in a dance.

At the end of the Cretaceous Period, the dinosaurs went away. There was some sort of catastrophic event...a meteor or volcano; we can only speculate.

Ohio was an upland during the Mesozoic Era. The rain washed the sand and dinosaur bones away. There is no evidence of them in our great state to this very day.

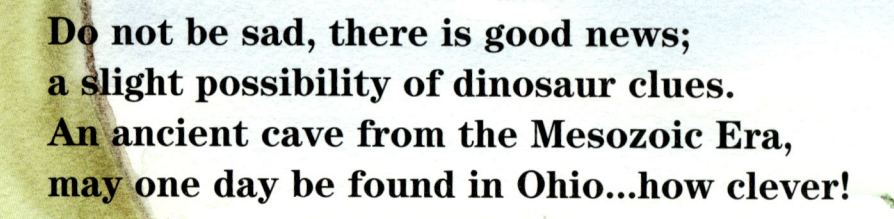

Do not be sad, there is good news;
a slight possibility of dinosaur clues.
An ancient cave from the Mesozoic Era,
may one day be found in Ohio...how clever!

Much of the bedrock is carbonate, limestone
and dolomite; which, to our glee, is susceptible
to the cave formation you see. Dinosaur remains
may be preserved in this way. We may find such
a cave in Ohio one day.

Perhaps it will be you, Little Buckeye, who finds lost dinosaur bones in Ohio. You never know. They may be buried under this big Buckeye tree. Until then, remember, there are living descendants of dinosaurs... one has just flown into our tree.

INDEX

**Dunkleosteus terrelli
(dunk-uhl-oz-tee-us) (tur-el-ee)**
Not a dinosaur, but a prehistoric armored fish. It measured between 18 and 30 feet long and swam in the shallow seas of Ohio during the Devonian Period. Lower jaw bone recovered from Highbanks Park, Ohio in 1987.

Meat eating dinosaur
Bipedal (walked on two legs), meat eaters that may have been warm blooded. They had light bones, powerful tails and huge skulls and jaws. They lived during the late Triassic to the late Cretaceous, all over the world.

Anchisaurus (ANG-kee-sawr-us)
This dinosaur walked on four legs but sometimes stood up and walked on two. Approximately 8 feet long, this dinosaur may have eaten meat and plants. It lived during the late Triassic and early Jurassic.

Rutiodon (ROOT-ee-o-don)
Originally thought to be a plant eater. A phytosaur (fye-toe-SAWR) not a dinosaur, but a meat eating reptile. It measured between 12 and 30 feet long, and looked very similar to crocodiles, but was not closely related. Rutiodon lived in lakes and streams during the late Triassic.

Coelophysis (see-lo-FYS-iss)
Standing approximately 3 feet tall at the hips and 10 feet long, it weighed about 100 pounds. This theropod is one of the earliest meat eaters known from the late Triassic.

Ammosaurus (AM-o-sawr-us)
This 7 foot long dinosaur had a small head, long neck and tail. Ammosaurus was an herbivore, and stood up on its hind legs to reach higher tree branches and leaves to eat. It lived during the Jurassic Period.

Camptosaurus (KAMP-to-sawr-us)
This dinosaur ranged in size from 4 feet to 17 feet long and was approximately 7 feet tall at the hips. It was an herbivore and lived in large numbers during the Jurassic Period.

Stegosaurus (STEG-o-sawr-us)
The most abundant plated dinosaur to ever be found in North America. It measured approximately 25 feet long and 11 feet tall at the hips. It was about the size of an Asian elephant. Stegosaurus was an herbivore. It is believed that the hollow plates on its back were used as a temperature regulator and not for protection from predators. Stegosaurus lived during the late Jurassic.

Apatosaurus (ah-PAT-o-sawr-us)
It is thought that this dinosaur was a plains dweller. Its immense length measured over 70 feet and it stood 15 feet high at the hips, weighing approximately 30 tons. Apatosaurus was a Sauropod from the late Jurassic.

Allosaurus (AL-o-sawr-us)
One of the best known carnosaurs. Allosaurus had teeth that measured from 2 to 4 inches long from the gum line. It was approximately 35 feet in length and 16.5 feet tall at the hips. It weighed approximately 4 tons and walked on two legs while using its tail for balance. It was a fierce predator and lived during the Jurassic Period.

Diplodocus (dih-PLOD-o-kus)
One of the longest dinosaurs ever found measuring approximately 90 feet long. It had a whiplike tail measuring 45 feet long and stood 13 feet tall at the hips, weighing approximately 25 tons. It was an herbivore and lived during the late Jurassic.

Nanosaurus (NAN-o-sawr-us)
This dinosaur was between 2 to 4 feet long and approximately 1.5 feet tall at the hips. It was about the size of a turkey. An herbivore, Nanosaurus lived during the Jurassic Period.

Triceratops (try-SAYR-ah-tops)
Unlike other horned dinosaurs, Triceratops did not travel in large herds, but in small family groups or alone. The hollow horns and frills on Triceratops may not have been used for protection from predators, but for sparing with other Triceratops for territory or mates. Some Triceratops bones have been recovered with marks in specific areas indicating Triceratops sparred with each other. This behavior would have been similar to how present day male deer behave when competing for mates or territory. This dinosaur measured approximately 25 feet long and 9.5 feet tall at the hips. Triceratops was an herbivore and lived during the late Cretaceous.

Pteranodon (tayr-AN-o-don)
Not a dinosaur but a tailless pterosaur (a flying reptile). On average, its body was about the size of a turkey and it had a wing span of about 27 feet (almost the length of a school bus). It weighed approximately 33 pounds. Its head was 6 feet long from the tip of the beak to the end of the crest on the back of its head. It was a flier and a glider in light wind. It may have had fur; most likely warm blooded. Pterandon lived during the late Cretaceous.

Tyrannosaurus (ty-RAN-o-sawr-us)
This huge carnosaur was approximately 45 feet long and stood over 18 feet high at the hips. Its teeth were between 3 and 6 inches long from the gum line and over 6 to 12 inches long when including the root of the tooth. There were approximately 50 teeth lining its massive jaw at any one time. Each tooth was replaced approximately every two years, hence the teeth varied in length from long to short, alternating almost every other tooth. A single Tyrannosaurus would have produced hundreds of teeth in its estimated 20 year lifetime. It was a much feared predator who lived during the late Cretaceous.

Parasaurolophus (par-ah-sawr-OL-o-fus)
This duckbill had a huge crest extending from the top of its head. The use of this hollow tube or crest measuring 5 feet in length is not known. Perhaps it was used as a horn for calling purposes or maybe as a mechanism to help it smell. It was approximately 30 feet long and stood 16 feet tall at the hips. This duckbill dinosaur was an herbivore, and lived during the late Cretaceous.

Pachycephalosaurs (pak-ee-sef-ah-lo-SAWR-us)
This dinosaur had a thick covering over its head. It was about 12 feet long and an herbivore. It has been speculated that it lived in herds and that the males competed for mates and territories by butting their heads together. This dinosaur lived during the late Cretaceous.